Project Management Simplified: A Practical Approach

No part of this publication may be reproduced, distributed, or transmitted in any form or by any means, including photocopying, recording, or other electronic or mechanical methods, without the prior written permission of the publisher, except in the case of brief quotations embodied in critical reviews and certain other noncommercial uses permitted by copyright law.

Copyright © 2024 Infowave MRV
All rights reserved.

Table of Content

Chapter 1: Introduction to Project Management

- Overview of project management principles and practices.

Chapter 2: Understanding Projects

- Defining what constitutes a project and its lifecycle.

Chapter 3: Project Initiation

- Identifying project goals, stakeholders, and feasibility studies.

Chapter 4: Project Planning

- Creating project plans, timelines, and resource allocation.

Chapter 5: Setting Objectives and KPIs

- Establishing clear objectives and key performance indicators.

Chapter 6: Risk Management

- Identifying, analyzing, and mitigating project risks.

Chapter 7: Team Formation and Roles

- Building effective teams and defining roles and responsibilities.

Chapter 8: Communication Management

- Strategies for effective communication among stakeholders.

Chapter 9: Task Management Techniques

- Tools and methods for managing tasks and deadlines.

Chapter 10: Budgeting and Cost Management

- Estimating costs and managing project budgets.

Chapter 11: Quality Management

- Ensuring quality standards and continuous improvement.

Chapter 12: Monitoring and Controlling Projects

- Techniques for tracking progress and making adjustments.

Chapter 13: Agile vs. Waterfall Methodologies

- Comparing and contrasting different project management approaches.

Chapter 14: Stakeholder Management

- Engaging and managing stakeholder expectations.

Chapter 15: Change Management

- Handling changes and adapting to new requirements.

Chapter 16: Project Documentation

- Importance of documentation and maintaining records.

Chapter 17: Closing Projects

- Steps for project closure and evaluation of outcomes.

Chapter 18: Lessons Learned and Best Practices

- Capturing lessons learned for future projects.

Chapter 19: Tools and Software for Project Management

- Overview of popular project management tools.

Chapter 20: The Future of Project Management

- Trends and innovations shaping the future of project management.

Chapter 1: Introduction to Project Management

What is Project Management?

Project management is the application of knowledge, skills, tools, and techniques to project activities to meet project requirements. It involves planning, executing, monitoring, controlling, and closing projects effectively and efficiently. The primary objective of project management is to achieve specific goals and deliverables within a defined scope, time, and budget.

Importance of Project Management

In today's fast-paced and dynamic environment, organizations face increasing challenges in delivering projects successfully. Effective project management is crucial for several reasons:

1. **Alignment with Strategic Goals:** Projects are often the means through which organizations achieve their strategic objectives. Proper project management ensures that projects align with business goals.
2. **Resource Optimization:** By effectively managing resources (human, financial, and material), organizations can maximize efficiency and minimize waste.

3. **Risk Mitigation:** Every project carries inherent risks. Project management helps identify potential risks early on, enabling teams to develop strategies to mitigate them.
4. **Stakeholder Satisfaction:** Understanding and managing stakeholder expectations is vital. Project management provides a structured approach to communication and engagement.
5. **Quality Control:** A focus on quality throughout the project lifecycle ensures that the deliverables meet or exceed expectations.

The Project Management Lifecycle

The project management lifecycle consists of five key phases:

1. **Initiation:** This phase involves defining the project at a high level, including objectives, scope, and stakeholders. A project charter is often created to formalize the project's approval.
2. **Planning:** Detailed planning is crucial for project success. This phase includes developing a project plan that outlines the tasks, timelines, resources, and budget. It also involves risk assessment and stakeholder engagement.
3. **Execution:** During execution, the project plan is put into action. This phase involves coordinating people and resources, managing stakeholder

engagement, and ensuring quality standards are met.
4. **Monitoring and Controlling:** Throughout the project, progress must be monitored against the plan. This phase includes tracking performance, identifying variances, and making adjustments as necessary to keep the project on track.
5. **Closure:** Once the project objectives have been met, the project is formally closed. This phase involves finalizing deliverables, obtaining stakeholder acceptance, and documenting lessons learned for future projects.

Key Components of Project Management

- **Scope:** The work required to deliver the project's outcomes. Clearly defining the scope helps prevent scope creep, which can lead to project overruns.
- **Time:** The schedule for completing project tasks and achieving milestones. Effective time management is crucial for meeting deadlines.
- **Cost:** The budget allocated for the project. Managing costs involves estimating, budgeting, and controlling expenses to ensure the project remains financially viable.
- **Quality:** The standards and criteria that project deliverables must meet. Quality management involves continuous monitoring and improvement.

- **Human Resources:** The people involved in the project. Effective team management is essential for fostering collaboration and ensuring productivity.
- **Communication:** The flow of information among stakeholders. Clear communication strategies are vital for keeping everyone informed and engaged.

Conclusion

Project management is a vital discipline that enables organizations to navigate the complexities of delivering projects successfully. By understanding the principles, processes, and best practices outlined in this book, readers will be equipped with the tools they need to simplify project management and drive successful outcomes. Whether you are a seasoned project manager or new to the field, embracing project management can enhance your ability to lead projects effectively, ensuring that they align with organizational goals and meet stakeholder expectations.

As we delve deeper into the subsequent chapters, we will explore each aspect of project management in detail, providing practical insights and strategies to enhance your project management skills.

Chapter 2: Understanding Projects

What is a Project?

A project is a temporary endeavor undertaken to create a unique product, service, or result. This definition emphasizes two key characteristics of projects:

1. **Temporary Nature:** Projects have a defined beginning and end. They are not ongoing; once the objectives are met, the project concludes.
2. **Unique Deliverables:** Each project aims to produce something distinctive. Whether it's a new product, a service enhancement, or an organizational change, the deliverables are specific to that project.

Characteristics of Projects

To better understand projects, let's explore their essential characteristics:

1. **Defined Objectives:** Projects are driven by specific goals. Clearly articulated objectives provide direction and a basis for measuring success.
2. **Scope:** The scope outlines what is included and excluded from the project. A well-defined scope helps prevent scope creep, ensuring that all stakeholders are aligned on expectations.

3. **Resources:** Every project requires resources—people, equipment, materials, and finances. Effective resource management is critical for project success.
4. **Constraints:** Projects operate within constraints such as time, cost, and quality. These constraints must be balanced to achieve the project objectives.
5. **Stakeholders:** Projects involve multiple stakeholders, including sponsors, team members, customers, and end-users. Understanding their needs and expectations is essential for success.
6. **Risk:** Every project carries inherent risks. Identifying and managing these risks is crucial for minimizing negative impacts on the project.

The Project Lifecycle

Projects follow a lifecycle that can be divided into distinct phases. While the number and names of these phases can vary, they generally include:

1. **Initiation:** This phase involves defining the project, identifying stakeholders, and obtaining necessary approvals. The project charter is often created during this stage to outline the project's purpose and objectives.
2. **Planning:** Detailed planning is conducted to outline how the project will be executed. This

includes developing schedules, resource plans, budgets, and risk management strategies.
3. **Execution:** In this phase, the project plan is put into action. Teams work on tasks to produce the project deliverables, and project managers coordinate efforts, ensuring that the project remains on track.
4. **Monitoring and Controlling:** Throughout execution, the project's progress is monitored. Key performance indicators (KPIs) are used to assess whether the project is on schedule, within budget, and meeting quality standards. Adjustments are made as necessary to address any deviations from the plan.
5. **Closure:** Once project objectives are achieved, the project is formally closed. This involves delivering the final product, obtaining stakeholder approval, and conducting a retrospective to document lessons learned for future projects.

Types of Projects

Projects can be classified into various types based on different criteria:

1. **By Industry:**
    - **Construction Projects:** Building structures like homes, offices, or infrastructure.

- **IT Projects:** Developing software applications or systems.
- **Marketing Projects:** Launching new marketing campaigns or products.

2. **By Complexity:**
   - **Simple Projects:** Low complexity, often with straightforward objectives and few stakeholders.
   - **Complex Projects:** Involve multiple interdependent tasks, diverse stakeholders, and higher risks.
3. **By Duration:**
   - **Short-term Projects:** Completed in a few weeks or months.
   - **Long-term Projects:** Extend over several months or years, often involving significant resources and planning.
4. **By Scope:**
   - **Internal Projects:** Focused on improving internal processes or systems within an organization.
   - **External Projects:** Involve delivering products or services to clients or customers.

The Role of a Project Manager

A project manager is responsible for leading and coordinating all aspects of a project. Key responsibilities include:

- **Planning and Scheduling:** Developing comprehensive project plans and timelines.
- **Team Leadership:** Guiding and motivating team members to achieve project goals.
- **Communication:** Facilitating effective communication among stakeholders.
- **Risk Management:** Identifying and mitigating potential risks throughout the project lifecycle.
- **Monitoring Progress:** Tracking project performance and making necessary adjustments to stay on course.

Conclusion

Understanding projects is fundamental to effective project management. By grasping the unique characteristics, lifecycle phases, and various types of projects, readers will be better prepared to tackle the challenges that arise in managing projects. In the following chapters, we will delve deeper into each phase of the project lifecycle and explore practical tools and techniques that can simplify project management, helping you achieve successful outcomes.

Chapter 3: Project Initiation

Project initiation is the first phase of the project management lifecycle, and it's where the groundwork for success is laid. This stage is critical because the decisions and plans made here will influence every subsequent phase of the project. By the end of the initiation phase, you will have a clear understanding of what the project entails, who is involved, and what success looks like.

The Importance of Project Initiation

Starting a project without proper initiation is like setting off on a journey without a map. A strong initiation process ensures that everyone is aligned on the project's purpose and objectives. When the foundation is strong, the project is far more likely to succeed. Remember, investing time in this phase can save you from costly errors and confusion later. You're setting the stage for success!

Key Elements of Project Initiation

1. **Defining the Project Goals and Objectives**
    - The first step in project initiation is to clearly define the project's goals. Why is this project being undertaken? What problem is it trying to solve, or what opportunity is it leveraging? Specific and

measurable goals give your project purpose and direction. When goals are clear, the path to success becomes easier to navigate.
- **Example:** If the project involves launching a new product, the goal might be to introduce it to the market within six months and achieve a 10% market share in the first year.

2. **Identifying Stakeholders**
   - Stakeholders are individuals or groups who have an interest in the project's outcome. They can include clients, team members, executives, suppliers, and end-users. Identifying your stakeholders early on helps ensure that their needs and expectations are considered from the start.
   - **Tip:** Creating a stakeholder analysis or mapping out key stakeholders can clarify their roles and influence on the project. Stay proactive in managing expectations—it's a great way to avoid miscommunication later!

3. **Creating a Project Charter**
   - The project charter is a document that formally authorizes the project. It outlines the project's purpose, objectives, scope, key stakeholders, and high-level timeline. A well-written charter

provides clarity and ensures that everyone is on the same page before the project begins.
- **Motivation:** Think of the project charter as your "project passport." It gives you the authority to proceed and helps you avoid misunderstandings down the road.

4. **Defining Scope**
    - The scope is a crucial component that determines what is and isn't included in the project. Defining scope early prevents scope creep, which happens when new tasks or objectives are added to a project without the necessary adjustments to resources or time.
    - **Tip:** A detailed scope document, outlining the project boundaries, deliverables, and exclusions, acts as your safety net. Stick to it, and you'll stay focused on your goals!

5. **Conducting a Feasibility Study**
    - A feasibility study is conducted to assess whether the project is realistic in terms of technical, financial, and operational aspects. This analysis helps you identify any obstacles before the project kicks off.
    - **Example:** If the project is to launch a new app, the feasibility study would examine whether the company has the technical

skills, budget, and market conditions necessary for success.
- **Positive Reinforcement:** Being thorough now can help avoid headaches later. You're taking proactive steps to ensure the project is set up for smooth execution—well done!

6. **Risk Identification**
   - Every project comes with potential risks. Identifying and documenting risks early on allows you to develop mitigation strategies that can prevent these risks from derailing your project. Risk management is an ongoing process, but the initiation phase is when you begin building your awareness.
   - **Tip:** Create a risk register to document risks, their potential impacts, and mitigation strategies. It's your first line of defense in maintaining control over the project.

Creating a Strong Project Team

Once you've established the groundwork for the project, it's time to form your team. Your team members are the heart of the project, and building the right team sets the tone for success.

- **Roles and Responsibilities:** Clearly define the roles and responsibilities of each team member. This ensures that everyone knows what's expected of them and reduces the likelihood of confusion or duplicated efforts.
- **Skills Assessment:** Choose team members whose skills align with the project's requirements. Consider both technical expertise and soft skills like communication, leadership, and collaboration.
- **Team Buy-In:** Encourage team members to take ownership of the project's objectives. When people are invested in the project's success, they're more likely to go the extra mile to achieve it.

Motivation: By selecting a strong team and ensuring clarity in roles, you're building a resilient foundation. Remember, a great project starts with great people—you've got this!

Obtaining Project Approval

Before the project can move into the planning phase, you'll need to secure formal approval. This approval typically comes from senior management or the project sponsor. During this stage, you present the project charter, scope, and any other relevant documentation to gain authorization to proceed.

Positive Outlook: This is your moment to shine! Presenting a well-thought-out project initiation plan is the key to gaining stakeholder confidence. You've already put in the hard work, so feel confident in presenting your vision.

Conclusion

Project initiation is more than just the starting point of your project—it's the blueprint for success. By clearly defining goals, identifying stakeholders, setting the scope, and conducting a feasibility study, you lay the groundwork for a well-executed project. Take your time in this phase, and remember, thorough preparation here will lead to smoother execution later. You're well on your way to mastering the art of project management—let's keep building on this momentum!

In the next chapter, we'll dive into project planning, where we'll explore how to turn your vision into an actionable plan. You're doing great—stay focused and positive!

Chapter 4: Project Planning

Project planning is a crucial phase in the project management lifecycle that transforms initial ideas and objectives into a detailed roadmap for execution. This chapter will explore the various aspects of project planning, emphasizing its importance in ensuring that projects are completed on time, within budget, and to the required quality standards.

The Importance of Project Planning

Effective project planning provides a framework for managing all aspects of the project. It serves as a guide for the project team and stakeholders, helping to ensure that everyone is aligned on objectives, timelines, and resources. Without a well-structured plan, projects are more likely to encounter delays, cost overruns, and misunderstandings among stakeholders.

Key Components of Project Planning

1. **Defining Project Objectives**
    - Clearly articulating the project goals is the first step in planning. Objectives should be Specific, Measurable, Achievable, Relevant, and Time-bound (SMART). For example, rather than stating "improve customer service," a SMART objective might be "reduce

customer service response time from 48 hours to 24 hours within three months."

2. **Developing the Project Scope**
   - The project scope outlines what is included and excluded from the project. It defines the deliverables and ensures that all stakeholders have a clear understanding of what to expect. A well-defined scope helps prevent scope creep—when additional tasks or features are added without proper evaluation.

3. **Creating a Work Breakdown Structure (WBS)**
   - A WBS is a hierarchical decomposition of the project into smaller, manageable components. It breaks the project down into tasks and subtasks, making it easier to assign responsibilities and track progress. For instance, if a project involves developing a new website, the WBS might include tasks like research, design, development, testing, and launch.

4. **Estimating Resources**
   - Estimating the resources required for each task is essential for effective planning. This includes determining the human resources needed (team members, skills), as well as physical resources (equipment, materials). Accurate resource estimation helps

ensure that the project can be completed without delays.

5. **Developing a Project Schedule**
   - A project schedule outlines when tasks will be completed and includes key milestones and deadlines. Techniques like Gantt charts or Critical Path Method (CPM) can be used to visualize the schedule and identify dependencies between tasks. Setting realistic timelines is crucial to keeping the project on track.

6. **Budgeting**
   - Establishing a budget involves estimating costs associated with resources, materials, and any other project-related expenses. It's important to create a detailed budget that aligns with the project scope and schedule. Budget management is an ongoing task throughout the project lifecycle.

7. **Risk Management Planning**
   - Identifying potential risks and developing mitigation strategies is a key component of project planning. Conducting a risk assessment helps to foresee possible challenges and prepare responses. A risk management plan should include the following:
     - Risk identification

- Risk analysis (impact and likelihood)
- Mitigation strategies

8. **Stakeholder Engagement**
   - Identifying and engaging stakeholders is crucial for project success. A stakeholder analysis helps determine who will be affected by the project, their interests, and how they should be engaged. Regular communication with stakeholders ensures that their expectations are managed and their input is considered.

9. **Communication Plan**
   - A communication plan outlines how information will be shared throughout the project. It specifies what information will be communicated, who will receive it, and the frequency of communication. Effective communication is key to keeping stakeholders informed and engaged.

10. **Quality Management Plan**
    - Defining quality standards and metrics is important for ensuring that the project deliverables meet expectations. A quality management plan should outline processes for quality assurance and quality control.

Creating the Project Management Plan

The culmination of the planning phase is the development of the Project Management Plan (PMP). This comprehensive document synthesizes all planning components, serving as the central reference point for the project. The PMP should include:

- Project objectives and scope
- Work breakdown structure
- Resource estimates
- Project schedule and milestones
- Budget and cost estimates
- Risk management plan
- Stakeholder engagement strategy
- Communication plan
- Quality management plan

Conclusion

Project planning is an essential phase that lays the foundation for project success. By carefully defining objectives, developing a comprehensive scope, estimating resources, and creating a detailed project schedule, project managers can navigate the complexities of project execution more effectively. The planning phase not only helps to identify potential challenges but also provides a clear roadmap for achieving the desired outcomes. In the next chapter, we will explore the execution phase, where the project plan is put into action, and the real work begins.

Chapter 5: Setting Objectives and KPIs

Setting clear objectives and key performance indicators (KPIs) is essential for project success. This chapter will delve into the importance of establishing objectives, the characteristics of effective objectives, and how to develop and utilize KPIs to measure progress and performance throughout the project lifecycle.

The Importance of Setting Objectives

Objectives provide direction and focus for the project team, ensuring that everyone is aligned on what needs to be achieved. Well-defined objectives:

1. **Guide Decision-Making:** Clear objectives help project managers and teams make informed decisions, prioritize tasks, and allocate resources effectively.
2. **Motivate Team Members:** When team members understand the project goals, they are more likely to feel motivated and committed to achieving them.
3. **Facilitate Measurement:** Objectives serve as benchmarks for measuring progress and success. Without clear objectives, it becomes challenging to assess whether the project is on track.

4. **Engage Stakeholders:** Well-articulated objectives help communicate the project's purpose to stakeholders, ensuring their support and involvement.

Characteristics of Effective Objectives

To be effective, project objectives should adhere to the SMART criteria:

1. **Specific:** Objectives should be clear and unambiguous. Instead of saying "improve customer satisfaction," specify "increase customer satisfaction scores by 15% within six months."
2. **Measurable:** There should be a way to quantify or assess progress toward the objective. This could be through metrics, surveys, or other forms of data collection.
3. **Achievable:** Objectives should be realistic and attainable. Setting overly ambitious goals can lead to frustration and demotivation.
4. **Relevant:** Objectives should align with broader organizational goals and be meaningful to stakeholders. They should contribute to the overall success of the organization.
5. **Time-bound:** Each objective should have a clear deadline for completion. For example, "reduce project delivery time by 20% by the end of Q4" provides a specific timeframe for assessment.

Developing Key Performance Indicators (KPIs)

KPIs are measurable values that demonstrate how effectively a project is achieving its objectives. They provide quantifiable metrics that can be monitored and analyzed. Developing effective KPIs involves several steps:

1. **Identify Critical Success Factors:**
    - Determine what is essential for the project's success. This could include factors like customer satisfaction, budget adherence, and schedule compliance.
2. **Align KPIs with Objectives:**
    - Each KPI should directly relate to a specific objective. For instance, if an objective is to increase sales by 20%, a relevant KPI might be the percentage increase in sales revenue over a specified period.
3. **Ensure KPIs are Measurable:**
    - KPIs should be quantifiable, allowing for easy tracking and reporting. Use data that is readily available and can be consistently collected.
4. **Set Targets:**
    - Establish target values for each KPI. For example, if a KPI is to achieve a customer satisfaction score of 90%, this target should be communicated to the team.

5. **Review and Adjust:**
    - Regularly review KPI performance and adjust targets as necessary based on project developments. This ensures that KPIs remain relevant and aligned with project goals.

Examples of Common KPIs

- **Schedule Performance Index (SPI):** Measures the efficiency of time utilization in a project. It is calculated as:

    $$SPI = \frac{EV}{PV}$$

    where EV is Earned Value and PV is Planned Value. An SPI of less than 1 indicates that the project is behind schedule.

- **Cost Performance Index (CPI):** Evaluates cost efficiency by comparing the budgeted cost of work performed to the actual cost. It is calculated as:

    $$CPI = \frac{EV}{AC}$$

    where AC is Actual Cost. A CPI of less than 1 indicates that the project is over budget.

- **Customer Satisfaction Score:** This can be measured through surveys and feedback

mechanisms, providing insight into how well the project meets stakeholder needs.
- **Quality Metrics:** These may include defect rates, number of revisions required, or adherence to quality standards.

Monitoring and Reporting

Once objectives and KPIs are established, it's important to implement a system for monitoring progress. Regularly tracking KPIs allows project managers to identify trends, make informed decisions, and adjust plans as necessary. Reporting on KPI performance should be transparent and shared with the project team and stakeholders to maintain accountability and foster collaboration.

Conclusion

Setting clear objectives and relevant KPIs is foundational for project management success. By adhering to the SMART criteria when defining objectives and developing measurable KPIs, project managers can guide their teams effectively and monitor progress throughout the project lifecycle. In the following chapters, we will explore additional elements of project management, including risk management and stakeholder engagement, to further enhance your understanding and skills in leading successful projects.

Chapter 6: Risk Management

Risk management is a critical aspect of project management that involves identifying, assessing, and mitigating potential risks that could affect project outcomes. This chapter will explore the principles of risk management, the risk management process, common types of risks, and strategies for effectively managing risks throughout the project lifecycle.

The Importance of Risk Management

Effective risk management is essential for project success for several reasons:

1. **Proactive Approach:** By identifying risks early, project managers can develop mitigation strategies before problems arise, reducing the likelihood of project delays and cost overruns.
2. **Improved Decision-Making:** A comprehensive understanding of potential risks allows project teams to make informed decisions about resource allocation, scheduling, and other critical factors.
3. **Stakeholder Confidence:** Demonstrating a proactive approach to risk management builds trust among stakeholders, showing that the project team is prepared to handle uncertainties.

4. **Enhanced Project Outcomes:** Effective risk management contributes to achieving project objectives by minimizing disruptions and ensuring that the project stays on track.

The Risk Management Process

The risk management process consists of several key steps, each crucial for developing a comprehensive risk management strategy:

1. **Risk Identification**
    - The first step in risk management is to identify potential risks that could impact the project. This can be done through various techniques, including:
        - **Brainstorming Sessions:** Engage the project team and stakeholders in discussions to generate a list of possible risks.
        - **Interviews:** Conduct interviews with key stakeholders to gather insights on their concerns and expectations.
        - **Checklists:** Utilize existing risk checklists from similar projects to ensure no common risks are overlooked.

- **SWOT Analysis:** Assess strengths, weaknesses, opportunities, and threats related to the project.
2. **Risk Assessment**
    - Once risks are identified, they must be assessed to understand their potential impact and likelihood. This involves:
        - **Qualitative Risk Analysis:** Prioritize risks based on their potential impact and likelihood using a scoring system (e.g., high, medium, low).
        - **Quantitative Risk Analysis:** For more complex projects, conduct quantitative analysis to estimate potential impacts on project objectives using statistical methods and modeling techniques.
3. **Risk Response Planning**
    - After assessing risks, develop strategies for addressing them. Common risk response strategies include:
        - **Avoidance:** Altering the project plan to eliminate the risk or protect project objectives from its impact.
        - **Mitigation:** Taking proactive steps to reduce the likelihood or impact of the risk.

- **Transfer:** Shifting the risk to a third party, such as through insurance or outsourcing.
- **Acceptance:** Acknowledging the risk and developing a contingency plan in case it occurs. This approach is often used for low-impact risks.

4. **Risk Monitoring and Control**
    - Risk management is an ongoing process. Regularly monitor identified risks and assess new risks as the project progresses. This includes:
        - **Risk Audits:** Periodically review the risk management plan to ensure its effectiveness and make adjustments as necessary.
        - **Status Meetings:** Include risk discussions in regular project meetings to keep the team informed and engaged.
        - **Update Risk Register:** Continuously update the risk register with new risks, changes in risk status, and results of risk response strategies.

Common Types of Risks

Understanding the types of risks that may affect a project can help in proactive risk management:

1. **Technical Risks:** These risks arise from the technology or technical aspects of the project, such as software bugs, integration issues, or equipment failures.
2. **Schedule Risks:** Risks that could affect the project timeline, such as delays in obtaining resources, dependencies on other projects, or unforeseen circumstances.
3. **Budget Risks:** These involve potential overruns due to underestimated costs, unexpected expenses, or changes in project scope.
4. **Resource Risks:** Risks associated with the availability and allocation of resources, including skilled personnel, materials, and equipment.
5. **Stakeholder Risks:** Risks that stem from stakeholder engagement, such as changing requirements, conflicts of interest, or lack of support.
6. **Regulatory Risks:** These arise from compliance with laws and regulations, including environmental laws, safety standards, and industry-specific regulations.
7. **Market Risks:** Risks related to market conditions, such as economic downturns, changing customer preferences, or increased competition.

Tools and Techniques for Risk Management

Several tools and techniques can aid in the risk management process:

1. **Risk Register:** A central document that lists identified risks, their assessments, and planned responses. It serves as a reference for the project team throughout the project lifecycle.
2. **Risk Matrix:** A visual representation that helps prioritize risks based on their likelihood and impact. It provides a clear overview of which risks require immediate attention.
3. **Scenario Analysis:** A technique that involves analyzing different scenarios and their potential impacts on the project. This helps teams prepare for various outcomes and develop appropriate responses.
4. **Decision Trees:** A visual tool used to map out different decision paths based on potential risks and their associated impacts, aiding in decision-making.

Conclusion

Risk management is an integral part of project management that helps ensure project success by proactively addressing uncertainties. By identifying, assessing, and developing strategies for potential risks, project managers can navigate challenges effectively and maintain control over project outcomes. In the following chapters, we will explore stakeholder engagement and communication strategies to further enhance your project management toolkit.

Chapter 7: Team Formation and Roles

Effective team formation is critical to the success of any project. A well-structured team, with clearly defined roles and responsibilities, can significantly enhance collaboration, productivity, and overall project outcomes. This chapter will discuss the importance of team formation, key considerations for assembling a project team, the various roles within a project team, and best practices for fostering a productive team environment.

The Importance of Team Formation

A well-formed project team lays the foundation for project success. Here are several reasons why effective team formation is essential:

1. **Diverse Skill Sets:** A successful project often requires a range of skills and expertise. A diverse team brings different perspectives and problem-solving approaches, enhancing creativity and innovation.
2. **Clear Accountability:** Clearly defined roles help establish accountability within the team. When team members know their responsibilities, they are more likely to take ownership of their tasks and contribute to the project's success.

3. **Effective Communication:** A well-structured team promotes better communication. Understanding who is responsible for what makes it easier to share information, discuss challenges, and collaborate effectively.
4. **Enhanced Morale:** A cohesive team that works well together fosters a positive work environment, boosting team morale and motivation.

Key Considerations for Assembling a Project Team

When forming a project team, consider the following factors:

1. **Project Requirements:** Understand the specific skills and expertise required for the project. This includes both technical skills (e.g., software development, design) and soft skills (e.g., communication, leadership).
2. **Team Composition:** Aim for a balanced team that includes individuals with complementary skills. Consider including team members with different levels of experience to promote knowledge sharing and mentorship.
3. **Availability:** Ensure that team members have the time and capacity to commit to the project. Assess their current workload and availability to avoid conflicts.

4. **Cultural Fit:** Consider the interpersonal dynamics of the team. A team with compatible values, work styles, and attitudes is more likely to collaborate effectively.
5. **Stakeholder Involvement:** Involve key stakeholders in the team formation process, especially if their expertise or input is critical to the project's success.

Common Roles in a Project Team

Each member of a project team plays a specific role that contributes to the overall success of the project. Here are some common roles and their responsibilities:

1. **Project Manager**
    - **Responsibilities:** The project manager is responsible for planning, executing, and closing the project. They lead the team, manage resources, communicate with stakeholders, and ensure that the project stays on track and within budget.
    - **Skills Required:** Strong leadership, communication, problem-solving, and organizational skills.
2. **Project Sponsor**
    - **Responsibilities:** The project sponsor provides support, resources, and guidance to the project manager and team. They represent the interests of

stakeholders and ensure that the project aligns with organizational goals.
- **Skills Required:** Strategic thinking, stakeholder management, and decision-making.

3. **Team Members**
   - **Responsibilities:** Team members execute the tasks and activities defined in the project plan. They collaborate to achieve project objectives and contribute their specific skills and expertise.
   - **Skills Required:** Varies based on role (e.g., technical skills, design skills, etc.) and effective communication.

4. **Business Analyst**
   - **Responsibilities:** The business analyst gathers requirements, analyzes business needs, and acts as a bridge between stakeholders and the project team. They ensure that the project delivers value to the organization.
   - **Skills Required:** Analytical thinking, communication, and understanding of business processes.

5. **Subject Matter Expert (SME)**
   - **Responsibilities:** SMEs provide specialized knowledge and expertise in a particular area relevant to the project. They help guide decision-making and

ensure that technical aspects meet industry standards.
- **Skills Required:** Deep knowledge of specific subject areas and effective communication.

6. **Quality Assurance (QA) Specialist**
    - **Responsibilities:** The QA specialist is responsible for ensuring that project deliverables meet quality standards. They develop and implement testing plans and identify any issues that need to be addressed.
    - **Skills Required:** Attention to detail, analytical skills, and knowledge of quality assurance processes.

7. **Communications Specialist**
    - **Responsibilities:** The communications specialist develops and executes the project communication plan. They ensure that information is shared effectively with stakeholders and that team members are informed of updates.
    - **Skills Required:** Strong written and verbal communication skills and experience in stakeholder engagement.

Best Practices for Fostering a Productive Team Environment

To create a collaborative and productive team environment, consider the following best practices:

1. **Establish Clear Goals and Expectations:**
    - Communicate project objectives and individual roles clearly. Ensure that everyone understands their responsibilities and how they contribute to the overall project goals.
2. **Encourage Open Communication:**
    - Foster an environment where team members feel comfortable sharing ideas, concerns, and feedback. Regular check-ins and open-door policies can enhance communication.
3. **Promote Collaboration:**
    - Use collaborative tools and platforms to facilitate teamwork. Encourage team members to work together on tasks, share knowledge, and support one another.
4. **Provide Support and Resources:**
    - Ensure that the team has access to the tools, resources, and training they need to succeed. Address any barriers that may hinder their ability to perform effectively.

5. **Recognize and Celebrate Achievements:**
    - Acknowledge individual and team accomplishments. Celebrating milestones fosters motivation and reinforces a positive team culture.
6. **Encourage Professional Development:**
    - Provide opportunities for team members to develop their skills and knowledge. This could include training, mentorship, or attending industry conferences.

Conclusion

Effective team formation and clearly defined roles are essential for successful project management. By assembling a diverse team with complementary skills and fostering a collaborative environment, project managers can enhance productivity and drive project success. In the next chapter, we will explore stakeholder engagement strategies and communication practices that further contribute to effective project management.

Chapter 8: Communication Management

Effective communication is a cornerstone of successful project management. It ensures that all stakeholders are informed, engaged, and aligned with the project goals. This chapter will explore the principles of communication management, the importance of stakeholder communication, tools and techniques for effective communication, and strategies for overcoming common communication challenges.

The Importance of Communication Management

1. **Alignment of Objectives:** Clear communication helps ensure that all stakeholders understand project objectives, roles, and responsibilities. This alignment is crucial for keeping the project on track.
2. **Stakeholder Engagement:** Regular communication fosters engagement and trust among stakeholders, which can lead to increased support and commitment to the project.
3. **Conflict Resolution:** Open lines of communication facilitate the early identification of conflicts or misunderstandings, allowing for prompt resolution and preventing escalation.

4. **Change Management:** Effective communication is essential for managing changes in the project scope, schedule, or resources. Keeping stakeholders informed helps minimize resistance to change.
5. **Knowledge Sharing:** A well-structured communication plan encourages the sharing of information and best practices, enhancing team collaboration and learning.

Key Components of Communication Management

1. **Communication Plan:**
   - A communication plan outlines how information will be disseminated throughout the project. It specifies:
     - **What information will be shared:** Project updates, meeting agendas, reports, etc.
     - **Who will receive the information:** Stakeholders, team members, clients, etc.
     - **How the information will be communicated:** Email, meetings, project management tools, etc.
     - **Frequency of communication:** Weekly updates, monthly reviews, etc.

2. **Stakeholder Analysis:**
   - Understanding the needs and preferences of different stakeholders is critical for effective communication. Conduct a stakeholder analysis to identify:
     - **Key stakeholders:** Individuals or groups with significant influence on the project.
     - **Information needs:** What information each stakeholder requires and how frequently they need updates.
     - **Preferred communication methods:** Identify the preferred channels for each stakeholder (e.g., email, phone calls, meetings).
3. **Message Clarity:**
   - Ensure that messages are clear, concise, and tailored to the audience. Avoid jargon and technical terms when communicating with non-experts. Use visuals, such as charts and graphs, to enhance understanding.
4. **Feedback Mechanisms:**
   - Establish mechanisms for collecting feedback from stakeholders. This can include surveys, suggestion boxes, or regular check-in meetings. Encourage

open dialogue and actively seek input to improve communication processes.

Tools and Techniques for Effective Communication

1. **Project Management Software:**
    - Utilize project management tools (e.g., Trello, Asana, Jira) to facilitate task assignment, progress tracking, and information sharing. These platforms allow team members to collaborate in real-time and keep everyone updated.
2. **Collaboration Tools:**
    - Tools like Slack, Microsoft Teams, or Zoom can enhance team communication, enabling quick discussions, video conferencing, and document sharing.
3. **Status Reports:**
    - Regular status reports provide updates on project progress, milestones, and challenges. These reports keep stakeholders informed and help track project health.
4. **Meeting Agendas and Minutes:**
    - Prepare clear agendas for meetings to ensure productive discussions. Document meeting minutes to capture key decisions, action items, and responsibilities, and distribute them promptly.

5. **Visual Communication:**
   - Use visual aids like Gantt charts, flowcharts, and dashboards to present complex information in an easily digestible format. Visuals enhance understanding and retention.

Strategies for Overcoming Communication Challenges

1. **Cultural Sensitivity:**
   - Be aware of cultural differences that may affect communication styles and preferences. Tailor your approach to accommodate diverse perspectives and practices.
2. **Time Zone Management:**
   - For teams working across different time zones, schedule meetings at convenient times for all participants. Consider recording meetings for those who cannot attend.
3. **Language Barriers:**
   - If working with multilingual teams or stakeholders, provide translation services or simplify language to ensure everyone understands the information.
4. **Managing Conflicts:**
   - Address conflicts or misunderstandings promptly. Use active listening and

empathy to understand differing viewpoints and find common ground.
5. **Regular Check-Ins:**
    - Schedule regular check-ins with team members and stakeholders to address concerns, provide updates, and reinforce communication channels. This builds rapport and keeps everyone engaged.

Conclusion

Effective communication management is vital for project success. By developing a comprehensive communication plan, understanding stakeholder needs, and utilizing appropriate tools and techniques, project managers can foster collaboration and engagement. Clear, open communication minimizes misunderstandings and enhances teamwork, ultimately contributing to achieving project objectives. In the next chapter, we will explore the importance of monitoring and controlling project progress and the tools available to help manage this process effectively.

Chapter 9: Task Management Techniques

Effective task management is crucial for ensuring that project activities are completed on time and within budget. It involves planning, organizing, and tracking tasks to achieve project objectives efficiently. This chapter will explore various task management techniques, their benefits, and how to implement them in your project management process.

The Importance of Task Management

1. **Clarity and Focus:** Clear task management helps team members understand their roles and responsibilities, allowing them to focus on their specific contributions to the project.
2. **Prioritization:** By organizing tasks based on urgency and importance, project managers can ensure that critical activities are addressed promptly, reducing the risk of delays.
3. **Resource Allocation:** Effective task management enables better allocation of resources, ensuring that the right skills and tools are available when needed.
4. **Progress Tracking:** Regularly monitoring tasks helps project managers identify potential issues early and make adjustments to keep the project on track.

5. **Enhanced Collaboration:** A structured approach to task management promotes collaboration among team members, fostering teamwork and communication.

Common Task Management Techniques

1. **To-Do Lists**
    - **Overview:** Simple yet effective, to-do lists outline tasks that need to be completed. They can be individual or team-based and provide a straightforward way to keep track of responsibilities.
    - **Implementation:** Create daily or weekly to-do lists, prioritizing tasks based on deadlines and importance. Use tools like digital apps (e.g., Todoist, Microsoft To Do) for easy access and updates.
2. **Kanban**
    - **Overview:** Kanban is a visual task management technique that uses boards to represent tasks and their statuses (e.g., To Do, In Progress, Done). This method enhances transparency and workflow management.
    - **Implementation:** Use a Kanban board (physical or digital) to visualize tasks. Team members move tasks across columns as they progress. Tools like

Trello or Asana can facilitate Kanban implementation.
3. **Gantt Charts**
   - **Overview:** Gantt charts provide a visual representation of the project timeline, illustrating tasks, durations, dependencies, and milestones. They help project manager's plan and track progress effectively.
   - **Implementation:** Create a Gantt chart using software like Microsoft Project or online tools like Smartsheet. Input tasks, assign durations, and define dependencies to visualize the project schedule.
4. **Time Blocking**
   - **Overview:** Time blocking involves allocating specific time slots for tasks or activities throughout the day. This technique helps improve focus and productivity by reducing distractions.
   - **Implementation:** Plan your day by blocking out time for specific tasks. Ensure to schedule breaks and allocate time for unexpected issues that may arise.
5. **Pomodoro Technique**
   - **Overview:** This time management technique involves working in short bursts (typically 25 minutes), followed by

short breaks. The goal is to maintain focus and productivity while preventing burnout.
- o **Implementation:** Set a timer for 25 minutes to focus on a task, then take a 5-minute break. After four cycles, take a longer break (15-30 minutes). Use apps like Focus Booster to manage this technique effectively.

6. **Task Dependencies**
   - o **Overview:** Understanding task dependencies involves identifying which tasks must be completed before others can begin. This helps in planning and prioritizing effectively.
   - o **Implementation:** Map out tasks and their dependencies using flowcharts or project management software. This visualization assists in scheduling and resource allocation.

7. **SMART Goals**
   - o **Overview:** SMART (Specific, Measurable, Achievable, Relevant, Time-bound) goals provide a framework for setting clear and achievable tasks. This technique helps ensure that tasks are well-defined and actionable.
   - o **Implementation:** For each task, define the criteria based on the SMART

framework. Ensure that each task aligns with broader project objectives.

8. **Daily Stand-Ups**
   - **Overview:** Daily stand-ups are brief meetings (usually 15 minutes) where team members share updates on what they accomplished, what they plan to work on, and any obstacles they face. This promotes accountability and communication.
   - **Implementation:** Schedule daily stand-ups at the same time each day. Keep the meetings focused and encourage concise updates from each team member.

Best Practices for Effective Task Management

1. **Prioritize Tasks:**
   - Use techniques like the Eisenhower Matrix to categorize tasks based on urgency and importance. Focus on high-priority tasks to maximize productivity.
2. **Set Clear Deadlines:**
   - Establish realistic deadlines for each task. Clear deadlines help team members manage their time effectively and ensure accountability.
3. **Monitor Progress:**
   - Regularly check the status of tasks and update team members on progress. Use

status reports or dashboards to provide visibility into task completion.
4. **Be Flexible:**
    - Be prepared to adjust tasks and priorities as project circumstances change. Flexibility allows the team to adapt to unforeseen challenges.
5. **Encourage Collaboration:**
    - Foster a collaborative environment where team members can support one another, share knowledge, and work together to complete tasks.
6. **Provide Feedback:**
    - Offer constructive feedback on task performance to help team members improve and stay motivated. Recognize achievements and celebrate milestones.

Conclusion

Effective task management techniques are essential for achieving project success. By implementing structured approaches, prioritizing tasks, and fostering collaboration, project managers can enhance productivity and ensure that project objectives are met. In the next chapter, we will explore monitoring and controlling project progress to ensure that projects stay on track and achieve desired outcomes.

Chapter 10: Budgeting and Cost Management

Budgeting and cost management are critical components of project management that ensure resources are allocated efficiently and project objectives are achieved within financial constraints. This chapter will explore the principles of budgeting, the process of cost management, techniques for effective budgeting, and best practices for monitoring and controlling project costs.

The Importance of Budgeting and Cost Management

1. **Resource Allocation:** A well-defined budget helps allocate resources effectively, ensuring that financial, human, and material resources are utilized optimally.
2. **Financial Control:** Effective cost management enables project managers to monitor expenses, identify variances, and take corrective actions to prevent budget overruns.
3. **Stakeholder Confidence:** A clear budget enhances transparency and builds trust among stakeholders, demonstrating that the project team is capable of managing resources responsibly.
4. **Decision-Making:** Accurate budgeting provides essential data for informed decision-making

regarding project scope, timelines, and resource needs.
5. **Project Viability:** Effective cost management ensures that the project remains financially viable, minimizing the risk of funding shortfalls or financial losses.

The Budgeting Process

The budgeting process involves several key steps, each vital for creating an accurate and effective project budget:

1. **Define Project Scope:**
    - Clearly outline the project's objectives, deliverables, and scope. Understanding the project scope is essential for estimating costs accurately.
2. **Identify Costs:**
    - Categorize project costs into direct and indirect costs:
        - **Direct Costs:** Expenses that can be directly attributed to the project, such as labor, materials, and equipment.
        - **Indirect Costs:** Overhead costs that are not directly tied to the project but necessary for its execution, such as utilities,

administrative expenses, and facility costs.

3. **Estimate Costs:**
   - Use estimation techniques to calculate costs for each component of the project. Common techniques include:
     - **Analogous Estimating:** Using historical data from similar projects to estimate costs.
     - **Parametric Estimating:** Applying statistical relationships between variables (e.g., cost per unit) to estimate costs.
     - **Bottom-Up Estimating:** Estimating costs for individual tasks and summing them to create the overall project budget.

4. **Develop the Budget:**
   - Compile cost estimates into a comprehensive budget that includes all expenses. Present the budget in a clear format, such as a spreadsheet or budgeting software.

5. **Obtain Approval:**
   - Present the budget to stakeholders for review and approval. Address any questions or concerns to ensure buy-in from key stakeholders.

6. **Baseline the Budget:**
   - Once approved, establish the budget as a baseline against which project performance will be measured. This baseline provides a reference point for monitoring and controlling costs throughout the project.

Cost Management Techniques

1. **Cost Control:**
   - Implement cost control measures to monitor expenses and ensure that they remain within the approved budget. This includes tracking actual costs against the budget and identifying variances.
2. **Earned Value Management (EVM):**
   - EVM is a project management technique that integrates scope, schedule, and cost. It provides a comprehensive view of project performance by measuring progress against the budget. Key metrics include:
     - **Planned Value (PV):** The budgeted cost of work scheduled to be completed by a specific date.
     - **Earned Value (EV):** The budgeted cost of work actually completed by a specific date.

- **Actual Cost (AC):** The actual costs incurred for work completed by a specific date.
    - By comparing these metrics, project managers can assess cost performance and forecast future performance.
3. **Variance Analysis:**
    - Regularly conduct variance analysis to compare planned costs to actual costs. Identify the causes of variances and implement corrective actions as needed. Common variance metrics include:
        - **Cost Variance (CV):** EV - AC (a positive value indicates that the project is under budget).
        - **Schedule Variance (SV):** EV - PV (a positive value indicates that the project is ahead of schedule).
4. **Contingency Planning:**
    - Set aside a contingency budget to address unforeseen costs or risks that may arise during the project. This budget provides flexibility and helps mitigate the impact of unexpected expenses.
5. **Change Management:**
    - Establish a change management process to evaluate and control changes that may impact project costs. All change requests should be assessed for their financial implications before approval.

Best Practices for Budgeting and Cost Management

1. **Engage Stakeholders:**
   - Involve key stakeholders in the budgeting process to ensure their needs and expectations are considered. This collaboration enhances transparency and buy-in.
2. **Be Realistic:**
   - Use realistic assumptions and estimates when developing the budget. Avoid underestimating costs or overpromising on deliverables.
3. **Monitor Regularly:**
   - Regularly review the budget and actual expenses throughout the project lifecycle. Frequent monitoring allows for timely adjustments and corrective actions.
4. **Communicate Effectively:**
   - Maintain open lines of communication with stakeholders regarding budget status, variances, and changes. Transparency fosters trust and facilitates informed decision-making.
5. **Document Lessons Learned:**
   - After project completion, document lessons learned related to budgeting and cost management. This information can provide valuable insights for future projects.

Conclusion

Budgeting and cost management are essential skills for project managers, enabling them to allocate resources effectively and ensure project success. By following a structured budgeting process, employing effective cost management techniques, and adhering to best practices, project managers can navigate financial challenges and keep projects on track. In the next chapter, we will explore monitoring and controlling project quality to ensure deliverables meet established standards and stakeholder expectations.

Chapter 11: Quality Management

Quality management is a vital aspect of project management that ensures deliverables meet specified standards and satisfy stakeholder expectations. This chapter will explore the principles of quality management, the quality management process, key techniques for ensuring quality, and best practices for maintaining high-quality standards throughout the project lifecycle.

The Importance of Quality Management

1. **Customer Satisfaction:** High-quality deliverables enhance customer satisfaction, leading to repeat business, referrals, and a positive reputation for the organization.
2. **Cost Reduction:** Effective quality management can reduce costs associated with rework, defects, and failures. By addressing quality issues early, organizations can avoid expensive corrections later.
3. **Compliance and Standards:** Adhering to quality standards and regulations helps organizations avoid legal and compliance issues, ensuring that products and services meet industry requirements.
4. **Risk Mitigation:** Quality management helps identify potential risks and issues related to

quality, enabling proactive measures to address them before they impact the project.
5. **Continuous Improvement:** A focus on quality fosters a culture of continuous improvement, encouraging teams to learn from experiences and enhance processes over time.

The Quality Management Process

The quality management process involves several key steps, each essential for achieving high-quality outcomes:

1. **Quality Planning:**
    - **Define Quality Standards:** Establish the quality standards and requirements for the project based on stakeholder expectations and industry norms.
    - **Develop a Quality Management Plan:** Create a comprehensive plan outlining how quality will be managed throughout the project. This plan should detail quality objectives, roles and responsibilities, and processes for quality assurance and control.
2. **Quality Assurance:**
    - **Process Improvement:** Focus on ensuring that processes are effective and efficient. Implement methodologies like Six Sigma

or Total Quality Management (TQM) to enhance process quality.
- **Training and Development:** Provide training to team members on quality standards, tools, and techniques. Continuous education enhances awareness and skills related to quality management.

3. **Quality Control:**
   - **Monitoring and Measuring:** Regularly monitor project deliverables to ensure they meet established quality standards. Use metrics and benchmarks to measure quality performance.
   - **Inspections and Testing:** Conduct inspections and testing of deliverables to identify defects and ensure compliance with quality standards. Implement acceptance criteria to evaluate whether deliverables are satisfactory.

4. **Quality Improvement:**
   - **Feedback Loops:** Establish mechanisms for collecting feedback from stakeholders and team members. Use this feedback to identify areas for improvement.
   - **Corrective Actions:** When quality issues are identified, implement corrective actions to address the root causes and prevent recurrence.

Key Techniques for Ensuring Quality

1. **Quality Metrics:**
    - Define and track key performance indicators (KPIs) related to quality. Common metrics include defect rates, customer satisfaction scores, and compliance rates. These metrics help assess quality performance and identify areas for improvement.
2. **Checklists:**
    - Use checklists to ensure that all quality requirements are met during the project. Checklists serve as reminders for critical tasks and help standardize processes.
3. **Flowcharts and Diagrams:**
    - Visual aids like flowcharts and diagrams can help map out processes and identify potential quality issues. These tools facilitate understanding and communication among team members.
4. **Root Cause Analysis:**
    - Implement techniques like the "5 Whys" or Fishbone Diagram to identify the root causes of quality issues. Understanding the underlying causes allows teams to develop effective corrective actions.
5. **Benchmarking:**
    - Compare project performance against industry standards or best practices.

Benchmarking helps identify gaps in quality and provides insights for improvement.
6. **Quality Audits:**
    - Conduct regular quality audits to evaluate adherence to quality standards and processes. Audits provide an objective assessment of quality management practices and identify areas for enhancement.

Best Practices for Quality Management

1. **Engage Stakeholders:**
    - Involve stakeholders in the quality management process to ensure their expectations and requirements are considered. Regular communication with stakeholders enhances understanding and alignment.
2. **Establish a Quality Culture:**
    - Foster a culture of quality within the project team. Encourage team members to take ownership of quality and emphasize the importance of delivering high-quality work.
3. **Document Processes:**
    - Maintain thorough documentation of quality management processes, standards, and results. Documentation

provides a reference for future projects and aids in continuous improvement.
4. **Train and Empower Teams:**
   - Provide ongoing training on quality management principles and techniques. Empower team members to identify and address quality issues proactively.
5. **Celebrate Successes:**
   - Recognize and celebrate achievements related to quality management. Acknowledging successes fosters motivation and reinforces the importance of quality within the team.

Conclusion

Quality management is essential for delivering successful projects that meet stakeholder expectations and industry standards. By implementing a structured quality management process, utilizing effective techniques, and adhering to best practices, project managers can enhance the quality of project deliverables. In the next chapter, we will explore the importance of stakeholder management and strategies for engaging and communicating with stakeholders effectively.

Chapter 12: Monitoring and Controlling Projects

Monitoring and controlling projects are essential components of project management that ensure projects stay on track, meet objectives, and adhere to established standards. This chapter will delve into the principles of project monitoring and controlling, the processes involved, key techniques for effective monitoring, and best practices for successful project oversight.

The Importance of Monitoring and Controlling

1. **Performance Measurement:** Monitoring project performance allows managers to assess whether the project is progressing according to plan and meeting established objectives.
2. **Early Detection of Issues:** Regular monitoring helps identify potential problems or deviations from the plan early, enabling timely corrective actions to prevent escalation.
3. **Resource Optimization:** By tracking resource usage and performance, project managers can optimize resource allocation and ensure efficient utilization.
4. **Stakeholder Communication:** Effective monitoring provides data and insights for regular

communication with stakeholders, fostering transparency and trust.
5. **Continuous Improvement:** The monitoring and controlling process provides valuable feedback that can be used to improve future projects and enhance project management practices.

The Monitoring and Controlling Process

The monitoring and controlling process involves several key steps:

1. **Establish Performance Baselines:**
    - **Scope Baseline:** Define the approved project scope, including deliverables, features, and requirements.
    - **Schedule Baseline:** Create a project schedule that outlines the timeline for task completion and milestones.
    - **Cost Baseline:** Develop a budget that includes all project costs, establishing a reference point for performance measurement.
2. **Collect Data:**
    - Use various data collection methods to gather information on project performance. This can include:
        - Progress reports from team members

- Timesheets and resource utilization reports
- Financial reports and expense tracking

3. **Analyze Performance:**
    - Compare actual performance against the established baselines to assess project health. Key metrics to consider include:
        - **Schedule Performance Index (SPI):** SPI = EV / PV (where EV is Earned Value and PV is Planned Value). An SPI less than 1 indicates the project is behind schedule.
        - **Cost Performance Index (CPI):** CPI = EV / AC (where AC is Actual Cost). A CPI less than 1 indicates the project is over budget.

4. **Identify Variances:**
    - Conduct variance analysis to identify differences between planned and actual performance. Key variance metrics include:
        - **Schedule Variance (SV):** SV = EV - PV (a positive value indicates the project is ahead of schedule).
        - **Cost Variance (CV):** CV = EV - AC (a positive value indicates the project is under budget).

5. **Implement Corrective Actions:**
   - When performance issues or variances are identified, develop and implement corrective actions to bring the project back on track. This may involve adjusting schedules, reallocating resources, or modifying project scope.
6. **Update Project Plans:**
   - Based on the analysis and corrective actions, update project plans as necessary. This includes revising schedules, budgets, and resource allocations to reflect the current state of the project.

Key Techniques for Effective Monitoring and Controlling

1. **Earned Value Management (EVM):**
   - EVM integrates scope, schedule, and cost to provide a comprehensive view of project performance. By analyzing the relationships between planned, earned, and actual values, project managers can assess overall project health and make informed decisions.

2. **Progress Reports:**
   - Regular progress reports provide stakeholders with updates on project status, achievements, challenges, and upcoming tasks. These reports enhance communication and keep stakeholders informed.
3. **Dashboards and Visualizations:**
   - Use project management dashboards to present key performance indicators (KPIs) and metrics visually. Dashboards provide real-time insights into project performance and facilitate quick decision-making.
4. **Risk Management:**
   - Continuously monitor identified risks and evaluate new risks that may arise during the project. Implement risk mitigation strategies and update the risk management plan as necessary.
5. **Change Control Process:**
   - Establish a formal change control process to evaluate and manage changes to project scope, schedule, and budget. This process helps assess the impact of changes and ensures that all stakeholders are informed and aligned.

Best Practices for Monitoring and Controlling Projects

1. **Establish Clear Communication Channels:**
   - Set up effective communication channels to facilitate information sharing among team members and stakeholders. Regular check-ins and status meetings promote transparency and collaboration.
2. **Involve Stakeholders:**
   - Engage stakeholders in the monitoring and controlling process. Their insights and feedback can provide valuable information for assessing project performance and making adjustments.
3. **Utilize Technology:**
   - Leverage project management software and tools to streamline data collection, analysis, and reporting. These tools can enhance accuracy and efficiency in monitoring project performance.
4. **Be Proactive:**
   - Anticipate potential issues and challenges before they arise. Proactive monitoring enables timely interventions and helps maintain project momentum.
5. **Document Lessons Learned:**
   - After project completion, document lessons learned related to monitoring and controlling processes. This information can inform future projects

and improve project management practices.
6. **Foster a Culture of Accountability:**
    - Encourage team members to take ownership of their tasks and responsibilities. A culture of accountability enhances performance and contributes to successful project outcomes.

Conclusion

Monitoring and controlling projects are critical activities that ensure project success by keeping performance aligned with established baselines. By implementing effective monitoring techniques, engaging stakeholders, and adhering to best practices, project managers can navigate challenges, make informed decisions, and achieve project objectives. In the next chapter, we will explore the importance of project closure and the steps involved in successfully closing a project.

Chapter 13: Agile vs. Waterfall Methodologies

Choosing the right project management methodology is crucial for the success of any project. Two of the most widely used methodologies are Agile and Waterfall. This chapter will explore the principles, characteristics, advantages, and disadvantages of both methodologies, helping project managers select the best approach for their specific project needs.

Overview of Waterfall Methodology

The Waterfall methodology is a traditional project management approach characterized by a linear and sequential process. It is named for its cascading effect, where each phase flows into the next, resembling a waterfall. The key phases of the Waterfall model typically include:

1. **Requirements Gathering:** Collect and document all project requirements from stakeholders before starting any design or development work.
2. **System Design:** Create a detailed design based on the gathered requirements. This phase outlines system architecture, user interfaces, and data structures.
3. **Implementation:** Develop the actual product based on the design specifications.

4. **Testing:** Conduct thorough testing to identify and fix any defects before the product is released.
5. **Deployment:** Release the completed product to users.
6. **Maintenance:** Address any issues or bugs that arise after deployment and make necessary updates.

Characteristics of Waterfall Methodology

- **Linear Process:** Each phase must be completed before the next one begins, making it easy to manage and track progress.
- **Documentation-Focused:** Extensive documentation is produced at each phase, providing a clear record of requirements, designs, and testing results.
- **Fixed Scope:** Changes to requirements are generally discouraged after the initial stages, as they can disrupt the entire project timeline.
- **Predictable Timelines:** Since the project follows a set sequence, timelines and budgets are often easier to estimate.

Advantages of Waterfall Methodology

- **Simplicity and Clarity:** The linear structure provides a clear roadmap for project execution,

making it easy for teams to understand their tasks and responsibilities.
- **Strong Documentation:** Comprehensive documentation ensures that all stakeholders are aligned on project goals, requirements, and designs.
- **Easier to Manage:** Project managers can easily monitor progress through each defined phase, making it straightforward to manage timelines and deliverables.
- **Best for Well-Defined Projects:** Ideal for projects with clear, unchanging requirements, such as construction or manufacturing.

Disadvantages of Waterfall Methodology

- **Inflexibility:** Once a phase is completed, going back to make changes can be time-consuming and costly.
- **Late Testing:** Testing occurs only after implementation, meaning defects or issues may not be identified until late in the project.
- **Assumes Predictability:** The model assumes that all requirements can be defined upfront, which is often not the case in dynamic projects.
- **Risk of Obsolescence:** By the time the project is completed, requirements may have changed, making the final product less relevant.

Overview of Agile Methodology

Agile methodology is an iterative and incremental approach to project management that emphasizes flexibility, collaboration, and customer feedback. Agile is particularly popular in software development but can be applied across various industries. The key principles of Agile include:

1. **Customer Collaboration:** Engaging with customers and stakeholders throughout the project to gather feedback and adapt to changes.
2. **Iterative Development:** Breaking the project into smaller iterations or sprints, each producing a potentially shippable product increment.
3. **Cross-Functional Teams:** Encouraging collaboration among team members with diverse skills and expertise.
4. **Adaptability:** Embracing changes in requirements, even late in the project, to enhance the final product's value.

Characteristics of Agile Methodology

- **Iterative Process:** Projects are divided into short cycles (sprints) that allow for frequent reassessment and adaptation.

- **Continuous Feedback:** Regular reviews and feedback loops ensure that the project aligns with customer needs and expectations.
- **Minimal Documentation:** Agile focuses on delivering working software over extensive documentation, although some documentation is still necessary.
- **Emphasis on Collaboration:** Team members work closely together, fostering open communication and teamwork.

Advantages of Agile Methodology

- **Flexibility and Adaptability:** Agile allows teams to respond quickly to changes in requirements or market conditions, ensuring that the project remains relevant.
- **Frequent Deliverables:** Regular iterations lead to earlier delivery of functional products, allowing stakeholders to see progress and provide feedback.
- **Improved Customer Satisfaction:** By involving customers throughout the process, Agile increases the likelihood that the final product meets their needs and expectations.
- **Enhanced Team Collaboration:** The collaborative nature of Agile promotes stronger relationships among team members and stakeholders.

Disadvantages of Agile Methodology

- **Less Predictability:** The iterative approach can make it challenging to predict timelines and budgets, especially in larger projects.
- **Scope Creep:** The flexibility to adapt to changes can lead to scope creep if not managed effectively, potentially derailing project objectives.
- **Requires Cultural Change:** Organizations may need to adapt their culture and processes to embrace Agile, which can be difficult for teams accustomed to traditional methodologies.
- **Documentation Challenges:** Minimal documentation may lead to misunderstandings or gaps in knowledge if team members leave or new members join.

Choosing Between Agile and Waterfall

When selecting a methodology, project managers should consider the following factors:

1. **Project Type and Complexity:** For projects with well-defined requirements and low uncertainty (e.g., construction), Waterfall may be more appropriate. For projects with evolving requirements (e.g., software development), Agile is often better suited.

2. **Stakeholder Involvement:** If frequent stakeholder feedback and collaboration are essential, Agile is preferable. If stakeholder requirements are clear from the outset, Waterfall may be more efficient.
3. **Timeline and Budget:** Consider how much flexibility is needed in timelines and budgets. Agile allows for more adaptability, while Waterfall provides predictability.
4. **Team Experience and Culture:** Assess the team's familiarity with each methodology and the organization's culture. Transitioning to Agile may require training and a shift in mindset.
5. **Risk Assessment:** Evaluate the level of risk involved in the project. Agile can help mitigate risks through regular feedback and iterations, while Waterfall may be more suitable for projects with lower risk.

Conclusion

Both Agile and Waterfall methodologies have their strengths and weaknesses, and the choice between them depends on the specific needs of the project. Understanding the fundamental principles, characteristics, advantages, and disadvantages of each approach enables project managers to make informed decisions that align with project goals and stakeholder expectations. In the next chapter, we will explore the importance of stakeholder management and strategies for effectively engaging and communicating with stakeholders throughout the project lifecycle.

Chapter 14: Stakeholder Management

Stakeholder management is a crucial aspect of project management that involves identifying, engaging, and communicating with individuals and groups who have an interest in or can influence the outcome of a project. Effective stakeholder management enhances project success by fostering collaboration, understanding needs, and addressing concerns. This chapter will explore the principles of stakeholder management, the stakeholder management process, techniques for effective engagement, and best practices for successful stakeholder communication.

The Importance of Stakeholder Management

1. **Building Relationships:** Strong relationships with stakeholders create a foundation for trust and cooperation, leading to smoother project execution.
2. **Understanding Needs and Expectations:** Engaging stakeholders helps project managers understand their needs and expectations, allowing for better alignment with project goals.
3. **Minimizing Resistance:** By involving stakeholders early and addressing their concerns, project managers can reduce resistance and foster buy-in for the project.

4. **Improving Decision-Making:** Stakeholders provide valuable insights and expertise, which can lead to more informed and effective project decisions.
5. **Enhancing Communication:** Effective stakeholder management promotes clear and transparent communication, ensuring that everyone is informed and aligned.

The Stakeholder Management Process

The stakeholder management process consists of several key steps:

1. **Identify Stakeholders:**
    - Create a comprehensive list of all individuals and groups who have a vested interest in the project. This includes internal stakeholders (team members, management) and external stakeholders (clients, suppliers, regulators).
    - Use stakeholder analysis techniques, such as a power/interest grid, to categorize stakeholders based on their influence and interest in the project.
2. **Analyze Stakeholders:**
    - Assess each stakeholder's interests, expectations, influence, and potential impact on the project. Understanding

these factors helps prioritize engagement efforts.
- Identify stakeholder needs and concerns to tailor communication and engagement strategies effectively.

3. **Develop a Stakeholder Engagement Plan:**
   - Create a stakeholder engagement plan that outlines how to interact with each stakeholder group. This plan should include:
     - Communication methods (meetings, emails, reports)
     - Frequency of communication
     - Key messages to convey
     - Responsibilities for stakeholder engagement

4. **Engage Stakeholders:**
   - Implement the engagement plan by actively communicating and collaborating with stakeholders. Foster open dialogue and encourage feedback to strengthen relationships.
   - Utilize various engagement techniques, such as workshops, surveys, and one-on-one meetings, to involve stakeholders effectively.

5. **Monitor and Manage Stakeholder Relationships:**
   - Continuously assess stakeholder engagement efforts and their impact on

project progress. Gather feedback to identify areas for improvement.
- Adjust engagement strategies as needed to address changing stakeholder needs, concerns, or project dynamics.

Techniques for Effective Stakeholder Engagement

1. **Stakeholder Mapping:**
    - Create a visual representation of stakeholders, categorizing them based on their influence and interest in the project. This map helps identify key stakeholders who require focused attention.
2. **Communication Plans:**
    - Develop tailored communication plans for different stakeholder groups, ensuring that messages are relevant and appropriate for their level of interest and influence.
3. **Regular Updates:**
    - Provide regular updates to stakeholders about project progress, milestones, and challenges. Keeping stakeholders informed fosters trust and encourages collaboration.
4. **Feedback Mechanisms:**
    - Establish mechanisms for gathering stakeholder feedback, such as surveys or

feedback forms. Actively seeking input shows stakeholders that their opinions are valued.
5. **Workshops and Collaborative Sessions:**
    o Organize workshops or collaborative sessions to engage stakeholders in discussions about project goals, challenges, and solutions. These interactions can enhance understanding and build relationships.
6. **Conflict Resolution:**
    o Address conflicts and disagreements promptly and constructively. Use negotiation and mediation techniques to resolve issues while considering stakeholders' perspectives.

Best Practices for Stakeholder Management

1. **Be Proactive:**
    o Engage stakeholders early in the project to build relationships and understand their needs and expectations. Proactive engagement helps identify potential issues before they escalate.
2. **Tailor Communication:**
    o Adapt communication styles and messages to suit different stakeholders. Consider their preferences, level of understanding, and areas of interest.

3. **Document Everything:**
   - Keep thorough documentation of stakeholder interactions, feedback, and decisions. This record provides valuable insights for future reference and helps maintain transparency.
4. **Foster a Collaborative Environment:**
   - Create an environment that encourages collaboration and open communication among stakeholders. Foster trust and respect to facilitate productive interactions.
5. **Show Appreciation:**
   - Recognize and appreciate stakeholders' contributions and efforts. Acknowledging their input fosters goodwill and encourages continued engagement.
6. **Evaluate and Adapt:**
   - Regularly assess the effectiveness of stakeholder management strategies and adjust as necessary. Continuous improvement ensures that stakeholder needs are met throughout the project.

Conclusion

Effective stakeholder management is essential for project success, as it fosters collaboration, understanding, and alignment among all parties involved. By following a structured stakeholder management process, employing effective engagement techniques, and adhering to best practices, project managers can build strong relationships with stakeholders and navigate challenges more effectively. In the next chapter, we will explore the importance of project closure and the steps involved in successfully closing a project.

Chapter 15: Change Management

Change management is a systematic approach to managing transformations in an organization or project. It involves preparing, supporting, and helping individuals and teams to adapt to changes in a way that minimizes resistance and maximizes benefits. In the context of project management, change management ensures that any alterations to project scope, timelines, or resources are effectively handled to maintain project integrity and achieve desired outcomes. This chapter will explore the principles of change management, the change management process, techniques for effective implementation, and best practices for managing change within projects.

The Importance of Change Management

1. **Facilitates Smooth Transitions:** Change management helps organizations navigate transitions effectively, ensuring that employees and stakeholders are prepared for changes.
2. **Minimizes Resistance:** By involving stakeholders and addressing their concerns, change management reduces resistance to change, leading to a smoother implementation process.
3. **Enhances Communication:** Effective change management fosters open communication, keeping stakeholders informed and engaged throughout the process.

4. **Increases Adoption Rates:** Well-managed changes result in higher adoption rates, as employees are more likely to embrace changes when they feel supported and informed.
5. **Improves Project Outcomes:** Change management ensures that changes are aligned with project goals, increasing the likelihood of successful outcomes.

The Change Management Process

The change management process can be broken down into several key steps:

1. **Identify the Change:**
    - Clearly define the nature of the change, its scope, and the reasons behind it. This could involve changes to project scope, timelines, resources, or organizational structures.
2. **Assess the Impact:**
    - Evaluate how the change will affect various stakeholders, processes, and outcomes. Consider both positive and negative impacts to understand the full scope of the change.
3. **Develop a Change Management Plan:**
    - Create a comprehensive plan that outlines how the change will be implemented. This plan should include:

- Objectives of the change
- Stakeholder analysis
- Communication strategy
- Training and support plans
- Implementation timeline

4. **Communicate the Change:**
    - Clearly communicate the details of the change to all stakeholders. Address the reasons for the change, its benefits, and how it will be implemented. Use various communication channels to reach different audiences.

5. **Engage Stakeholders:**
    - Involve stakeholders in the change process to foster ownership and support. Encourage feedback and address any concerns to build trust and collaboration.

6. **Implement the Change:**
    - Execute the change according to the change management plan. Ensure that resources are allocated effectively and that team members are equipped to handle the transition.

7. **Monitor and Evaluate:**
    - Continuously monitor the implementation of the change to assess its effectiveness. Gather feedback from stakeholders and measure key performance indicators (KPIs) to evaluate success.

8. **Adjust as Needed:**
    - Be prepared to make adjustments based on feedback and performance metrics. Flexibility is essential to address any unforeseen challenges and ensure successful adoption.

Techniques for Effective Change Management

1. **Change Impact Assessment:**
    - Conduct a thorough assessment to identify how the change will impact various stakeholders, processes, and systems. This helps prioritize engagement efforts and resource allocation.
2. **Stakeholder Engagement:**
    - Actively involve stakeholders in the change process through workshops, meetings, and feedback sessions. Their input can provide valuable insights and foster a sense of ownership.
3. **Training and Support:**
    - Offer training and resources to help employees adapt to the change. Providing support enhances confidence and skills, facilitating smoother transitions.

4. **Feedback Mechanisms:**
    - Establish channels for ongoing feedback throughout the change process. Regularly solicit input from stakeholders to gauge their concerns and make necessary adjustments.
5. **Change Champions:**
    - Identify and empower change champions within the organization. These individuals can advocate for the change, provide support, and help others navigate the transition.

Best Practices for Change Management

1. **Clear Vision and Goals:**
    - Establish a clear vision and set specific goals for the change initiative. Communicate these to all stakeholders to create alignment and focus.
2. **Involve Leadership:**
    - Secure buy-in from leadership and ensure their active involvement in the change process. Leaders set the tone for the organization and can influence employee attitudes toward change.
3. **Communicate Transparently:**
    - Maintain open and honest communication throughout the change process. Address concerns and provide

updates to keep stakeholders informed and engaged.
4. **Celebrate Successes:**
   - Acknowledge and celebrate milestones and successes during the change process. Recognizing achievements fosters motivation and reinforces positive behaviors.
5. **Document and Learn:**
   - Keep thorough documentation of the change process, including lessons learned and best practices. This information can inform future change initiatives and improve overall change management practices.
6. **Evaluate and Reflect:**
   - After the change has been implemented, conduct a thorough evaluation to assess its effectiveness and impact. Reflect on what worked well and what could be improved for future changes.

Conclusion

Change management is a vital component of project management that enables organizations to navigate transitions effectively. By following a structured change management process, employing effective techniques, and adhering to best practices, project managers can minimize resistance, enhance communication, and increase the likelihood of successful outcomes. In the next chapter, we will explore the importance of project closure and the steps involved in successfully closing a project.

Chapter 16: Project Documentation

Project documentation is a critical aspect of project management that involves creating, maintaining, and organizing documents that provide a record of the project's progress, decisions, and outcomes. Effective documentation ensures transparency, facilitates communication, and supports knowledge transfer throughout the project lifecycle. This chapter will explore the types of project documentation, their importance, best practices for creating effective documentation, and tools that can aid in the documentation process.

The Importance of Project Documentation

1. **Ensures Clarity and Consistency:** Documentation provides a clear and consistent reference for project objectives, requirements, and processes, helping all stakeholders stay aligned.
2. **Facilitates Communication:** Well-organized documentation promotes effective communication among team members, stakeholders, and management, reducing misunderstandings and miscommunications.
3. **Supports Decision-Making:** Documentation captures important decisions, rationale, and changes, providing a reference for future decision-making and ensuring that everyone is informed.

4. **Enhances Accountability:** Clear documentation assigns responsibilities and outlines expectations, holding team members accountable for their roles and tasks.
5. **Provides a Knowledge Base:** Documenting lessons learned and best practices supports organizational learning and helps future projects benefit from past experiences.
6. **Regulatory Compliance:** For many industries, maintaining thorough documentation is essential for compliance with regulations and standards.

Types of Project Documentation

1. **Project Charter:**
    - A formal document that authorizes the project, outlines its objectives, and defines the roles and responsibilities of stakeholders.
2. **Project Plan:**
    - A comprehensive document that outlines the project's scope, objectives, timelines, resources, budget, and risk management strategies.
3. **Requirements Document:**
    - A detailed description of the project requirements, including functional and non-functional requirements, which

serve as the foundation for project deliverables.
4. **Stakeholder Analysis:**
    - A document that identifies project stakeholders, their interests, influence, and engagement strategies.
5. **Risk Management Plan:**
    - A document that outlines the approach to identifying, assessing, and mitigating project risks.
6. **Meeting Minutes:**
    - Records of discussions, decisions, and action items from project meetings, serving as a reference for future discussions and follow-ups.
7. **Status Reports:**
    - Regular updates that provide an overview of project progress, milestones achieved, challenges faced, and upcoming tasks.
8. **Change Requests:**
    - Documents that outline proposed changes to the project scope, timelines, or resources, along with their rationale and impact assessments.
9. **Lessons Learned Document:**
    - A record of insights and experiences gained throughout the project, including what worked well and what could be improved for future projects.

10. **Final Project Report:**
    - A comprehensive summary of the project, including achievements, challenges, and recommendations for future initiatives.

Best Practices for Effective Project Documentation

1. **Be Clear and Concise:**
    - Use clear and straightforward language to ensure that documentation is easily understood by all stakeholders. Avoid jargon and technical terms unless necessary.
2. **Use Consistent Formatting:**
    - Maintain consistent formatting and structure across all project documents to enhance readability and facilitate navigation.
3. **Keep Documentation Up to Date:**
    - Regularly review and update documents to reflect current project status, changes, and lessons learned. Outdated documentation can lead to confusion and misalignment.
4. **Organize Documentation:**
    - Implement a systematic approach to organizing documentation, such as using folders, labels, or a document management system, to make it easy for

team members to find relevant information.
5. **Involve Stakeholders:**
    o Engage stakeholders in the documentation process by seeking their input and feedback. This collaboration ensures that documents accurately reflect their perspectives and needs.
6. **Establish Version Control:**
    o Use version control to track changes to documents over time. This practice helps maintain a clear record of revisions and ensures that team members are using the most current versions.
7. **Leverage Technology:**
    o Utilize project management tools and software that facilitate documentation, collaboration, and version control. Many tools offer templates and features to streamline the documentation process.
8. **Train Team Members:**
    o Provide training on documentation best practices and tools to ensure that all team members understand their roles in maintaining accurate and effective documentation.
9. **Document Decisions:**
    o Record important decisions, including the rationale behind them, to create a clear

history that can inform future decision-making and project evaluations.
10. **Create a Documentation Plan:**
    o Develop a plan that outlines the types of documents to be created, responsibilities for documentation, and timelines for updates. This plan serves as a roadmap for effective documentation practices.

Tools for Project Documentation

1. **Document Management Systems (DMS):**
   o Software that provides a centralized repository for storing, organizing, and managing project documents. Examples include SharePoint, Google Drive, and Dropbox.
2. **Project Management Software:**
   o Tools like Asana, Trello, and Jira offer built-in features for documentation, collaboration, and tracking project progress.
3. **Collaboration Platforms:**
   o Platforms such as Microsoft Teams or Slack facilitate real-time communication and collaboration, making it easy to share and discuss project documents.
4. **Version Control Systems:**
   o Tools like Git help track changes to documents and code, ensuring that all

team members are working with the latest versions.

5. **Templates:**
    - Use standardized templates for common project documents to ensure consistency and save time in the documentation process.

Conclusion

Effective project documentation is essential for successful project management. By creating and maintaining clear, organized, and up-to-date documentation, project managers can enhance communication, support decision-making, and facilitate knowledge transfer. Adopting best practices and leveraging appropriate tools can significantly improve the quality and efficiency of project documentation. In the next chapter, we will explore the importance of project closure and the steps involved in successfully closing a project.

Chapter 17: Closing Projects

Closing a project is a critical phase in project management that involves finalizing all project activities, ensuring that project deliverables meet requirements, and officially closing the project. This phase is essential for assessing the project's success, documenting lessons learned, and ensuring that all stakeholders are aligned before the project is considered complete. This chapter will explore the importance of project closure, the steps involved in closing a project, key deliverables, and best practices for a successful project closure.

The Importance of Project Closure

1. **Formal Completion:** Closing a project formally acknowledges its completion, providing clarity to stakeholders and team members about the project's status.
2. **Assessment of Success:** The closure phase allows project managers to evaluate whether the project met its objectives, adhered to the budget, and satisfied stakeholder expectations.
3. **Documentation of Lessons Learned:** Reflecting on the project experience helps capture valuable insights and lessons learned, which can inform future projects and improve organizational practices.

4. **Resource Reallocation:** Properly closing a project frees up resources, including team members, budget, and equipment, allowing them to be allocated to new initiatives.
5. **Stakeholder Satisfaction:** A successful closure ensures that stakeholders are satisfied with the project outcomes, reinforcing relationships and building trust for future collaborations.

Steps Involved in Closing a Project

1. **Review Project Deliverables:**
    - Ensure that all project deliverables have been completed, reviewed, and meet the quality standards specified in the project plan. Confirm that deliverables align with stakeholder expectations.
2. **Obtain Formal Acceptance:**
    - Secure formal acceptance of the project deliverables from stakeholders or clients. This often involves obtaining sign-offs that indicate satisfaction with the results.
3. **Conduct Final Project Review:**
    - Organize a final project review meeting with the project team and key stakeholders. Discuss project outcomes, performance against objectives, and any challenges faced during execution.

4. **Document Lessons Learned:**
   o Create a lessons learned document that captures insights from the project. Include what worked well, what did not, and recommendations for future projects. This document serves as a knowledge base for the organization.
5. **Complete Final Reports:**
   o Prepare a final project report that summarizes the project, including objectives, outcomes, budget, timeline, and lessons learned. This report provides a comprehensive overview for stakeholders and serves as a historical record.
6. **Release Project Resources:**
   o Release team members, equipment, and other resources involved in the project. Communicate with the team about their next steps and provide support for their transition to new roles or projects.
7. **Archive Project Documentation:**
   o Organize and store all project documentation, including plans, reports, communications, and lessons learned, in a central repository for future reference. Ensure that the documentation is accessible to relevant stakeholders.

8. **Celebrate Success:**
   - Acknowledge and celebrate the team's efforts and achievements. Recognizing hard work fosters team morale and reinforces a culture of appreciation within the organization.
9. **Conduct a Closure Meeting:**
   - Hold a closure meeting with the project team and key stakeholders to review the project's success, discuss the lessons learned document, and share final thoughts. This meeting reinforces closure and allows for open communication.
10. **Follow Up with Stakeholders:**
    - After the project is closed, follow up with stakeholders to gather feedback on the project outcomes and the closure process. This feedback can provide valuable insights for future projects.

Key Deliverables in Project Closure

1. **Final Project Report:**
   - A comprehensive document summarizing the project's objectives, outcomes, budget, timeline, and lessons learned.
2. **Lessons Learned Document:**
   - A record of insights gained during the project, including successful strategies and areas for improvement.

3. **Formal Acceptance Sign-Off:**
   - Documentation indicating that stakeholders accept the project deliverables and outcomes.
4. **Archived Documentation:**
   - A collection of all project documentation, organized for future reference and knowledge sharing.
5. **Resource Release Documentation:**
   - Records indicating the release of project resources, including personnel and materials.

Best Practices for Successful Project Closure

1. **Plan for Closure Early:**
   - Integrate closure planning into the project plan from the outset. Consider the closure activities and deliverables during project execution to ensure a smooth transition.
2. **Communicate Clearly:**
   - Maintain open communication with stakeholders throughout the closure process. Keep them informed of final outcomes, lessons learned, and any follow-up actions.

3. **Engage the Team:**
   - Involve the project team in the closure process, including documenting lessons learned and preparing final reports. Their insights are valuable and help foster a sense of ownership.
4. **Be Thorough and Detailed:**
   - Ensure that all closure activities are completed thoroughly. This includes reviewing all deliverables, obtaining sign-offs, and archiving documentation.
5. **Reflect on the Project Experience:**
   - Take time to reflect on the project experience, including successes and challenges. This reflection fosters continuous improvement and enhances future project management practices.
6. **Celebrate Achievements:**
   - Acknowledge the hard work and achievements of the project team. Celebrating successes strengthens team relationships and encourages a positive work environment.
7. **Follow Up Post-Closure:**
   - After the project is closed, consider scheduling follow-up meetings with stakeholders to discuss the project's impact and gather feedback. This follow-up demonstrates commitment to continuous improvement.

Conclusion

Closing a project is a vital phase that ensures a formal end to project activities while capturing insights and lessons for future endeavors. By following a structured closure process, project managers can evaluate success, document valuable lessons learned, and facilitate resource reallocation. Emphasizing communication, thoroughness, and team involvement will lead to a successful project closure and set the stage for future project successes. In the next chapter, we will explore the importance of continuous improvement in project management and strategies for fostering a culture of learning and adaptation within organizations.

Chapter 18: Lessons Learned and Best Practices

In the realm of project management, capturing lessons learned and establishing best practices are essential components for fostering continuous improvement and enhancing future project success. This chapter will explore the significance of lessons learned, the process of documenting and analyzing them, the identification of best practices, and strategies for effectively implementing these insights within an organization.

The Importance of Lessons Learned

1. **Enhancing Future Projects:** Lessons learned provide valuable insights into what worked well and what did not during a project, guiding teams in improving processes and decision-making in future initiatives.
2. **Avoiding Repetition of Mistakes:** By documenting challenges and failures, organizations can avoid repeating the same mistakes, thereby increasing project efficiency and success rates.
3. **Knowledge Sharing:** Lessons learned foster a culture of knowledge sharing, allowing team members to learn from each other's experiences and expertise.

4. **Building a Knowledge Base:** A comprehensive repository of lessons learned serves as a reference for current and future projects, helping teams leverage past experiences.
5. **Improving Team Morale:** Acknowledging successes and learning from failures can boost team morale and foster a sense of accomplishment and resilience.

The Process of Documenting Lessons Learned

1. **Identify Key Moments:**
   - Throughout the project lifecycle, identify significant events, challenges, and successes that provide valuable insights. This can include project milestones, critical decisions, and unexpected issues.
2. **Gather Feedback:**
   - Engage project team members and stakeholders in discussions about their experiences during the project. Use surveys, interviews, or workshops to collect diverse perspectives on what went well and what could be improved.
3. **Document Insights:**
   - Create a structured lessons learned document that captures insights in a clear and organized manner. Include the following elements:

- **Event Description:** A brief overview of the event or situation.
- **What Worked Well:** Positive aspects and successful strategies that contributed to project success.
- **What Did Not Work:** Challenges, obstacles, and mistakes encountered during the project.
- **Recommendations:** Suggested actions or changes to improve future projects.

4. **Analyze Trends:**
   - Review documented lessons learned to identify recurring themes, patterns, or trends. Analyzing these insights helps teams understand broader issues and opportunities for improvement.
5. **Share and Disseminate:**
   - Share the lessons learned document with relevant stakeholders, including project teams, management, and future project managers. Consider using workshops or presentations to facilitate discussions around key insights.

Identifying Best Practices

1. **Evaluate Success Factors:**
   - Identify the factors that contributed to successful project outcomes. This may include effective communication

strategies, risk management techniques, or team collaboration practices.

2. **Assess Methodologies:**
   - Review the methodologies and frameworks used during the project. Determine which approaches were effective and could be standardized across future projects.

3. **Incorporate Stakeholder Feedback:**
   - Gather feedback from stakeholders about their experiences and satisfaction with the project processes. Their insights can help identify practices that enhance collaboration and engagement.

4. **Develop Standard Operating Procedures:**
   - Create standard operating procedures (SOPs) based on identified best practices. These SOPs can serve as guidelines for project teams, ensuring consistency and efficiency in project execution.

5. **Establish Metrics for Success:**
   - Define metrics to measure the effectiveness of best practices. Regularly assess performance against these metrics to ensure continuous improvement.

Strategies for Implementing Lessons Learned and Best Practices

1. **Create a Central Repository:**
    - Establish a centralized repository for storing lessons learned and best practices. This could be an online database, intranet site, or document management system that is easily accessible to all team members.
2. **Incorporate into Project Management Processes:**
    - Integrate lessons learned and best practices into the project management lifecycle. Ensure that project teams review and reference these documents during project planning, execution, and closure.
3. **Conduct Regular Review Meetings:**
    - Schedule regular meetings to review lessons learned and best practices with project teams. Encourage open discussions about how these insights can be applied to current projects.
4. **Train and Educate Team Members:**
    - Provide training sessions to educate team members about the importance of lessons learned and best practices. Emphasize how these insights can

improve project outcomes and foster a culture of continuous improvement.
5. **Encourage a Culture of Learning:**
    - Foster a culture that encourages team members to share their experiences and insights openly. Recognize and reward individuals who contribute to the lessons learned process, reinforcing the value of knowledge sharing.
6. **Monitor and Evaluate Implementation:**
    - Regularly assess the effectiveness of implemented lessons learned and best practices. Gather feedback from project teams and stakeholders to identify areas for improvement and adjust strategies as needed.

Conclusion

Capturing lessons learned and establishing best practices are vital for enhancing project management capabilities and driving continuous improvement. By systematically documenting insights, sharing knowledge, and implementing effective strategies, organizations can create a culture of learning that leads to greater project success. As teams reflect on their experiences and adapt their approaches, they position themselves for future achievements and innovations. In the next chapter, we will explore the role of project management software and tools in enhancing project execution and collaboration.

Chapter 19: Tools and Software for Project Management

In the modern project management landscape, tools and software play a crucial role in facilitating planning, collaboration, tracking, and reporting. The right tools can enhance efficiency, improve communication, and streamline project workflows. This chapter will explore various categories of project management tools, their key features, popular software options, and tips for selecting the right tools for your projects.

The Importance of Project Management Tools

1. **Improved Collaboration:** Tools enhance communication among team members, enabling real-time collaboration, information sharing, and feedback.
2. **Efficient Planning and Scheduling:** Project management software allows teams to create detailed project plans, set timelines, and allocate resources effectively.
3. **Enhanced Tracking and Reporting:** Tools provide the ability to track progress, monitor key performance indicators (KPIs), and generate reports for stakeholders.
4. **Resource Management:** Software helps project managers allocate resources efficiently, balancing workloads and minimizing bottlenecks.

5. **Risk Management:** Project management tools can assist in identifying, assessing, and managing risks, ensuring proactive responses to potential issues.
6. **Centralized Documentation:** Many tools offer a central repository for project documentation, making it easy for team members to access relevant information.

Categories of Project Management Tools

1. **Project Planning Tools:**
    - These tools assist in creating project plans, defining tasks, and establishing timelines. They often include Gantt charts, work breakdown structures (WBS), and task dependencies.
    - **Popular Tools:** Microsoft Project, Smartsheet, TeamGantt.
2. **Collaboration and Communication Tools:**
    - These tools facilitate real-time communication, file sharing, and collaboration among team members. They may include chat features, video conferencing, and project forums.
    - **Popular Tools:** Slack, Microsoft Teams, Zoom, Google Workspace.
3. **Task Management Tools:**
    - These tools focus on managing individual tasks, assigning responsibilities, and

tracking progress. They help teams prioritize work and maintain accountability.
    - **Popular Tools:** Asana, Trello, Monday.com, ClickUp.
4. **Time Tracking and Reporting Tools:**
    - Time tracking tools help teams monitor time spent on tasks and projects. They often provide reporting features to analyze productivity and resource utilization.
    - **Popular Tools:** Harvest, Toggl, Clockify.
5. **Risk Management Tools:**
    - These tools assist in identifying, assessing, and managing risks throughout the project lifecycle. They often include risk registers and risk assessment matrices.
    - **Popular Tools:** RiskyProject, @RISK, RiskWatch.
6. **Resource Management Tools:**
    - Resource management tools help project managers allocate resources effectively, track availability, and balance workloads across teams.
    - **Popular Tools:** Resource Guru, Float, 10,000ft.
7. **Portfolio Management Tools:**
    - These tools provide a high-level overview of multiple projects, allowing

organizations to prioritize initiatives, allocate resources, and track overall performance.
- **Popular Tools:** Microsoft Project Online, Planview, Clarizen.

8. **Document Management Tools:**
   - Document management tools enable teams to create, share, and store project-related documents in a centralized location.
   - **Popular Tools:** SharePoint, Google Drive, Dropbox.

Key Features to Look for in Project Management Tools

1. **User-Friendly Interface:**
   - The tool should be easy to navigate, with an intuitive design that minimizes the learning curve for team members.
2. **Customizability:**
   - Look for tools that allow customization to fit your team's specific workflows, processes, and reporting needs.
3. **Collaboration Features:**
   - Ensure the tool supports real-time collaboration, file sharing, and communication among team members.
4. **Reporting and Analytics:**
   - Choose tools that provide robust reporting capabilities, allowing you to

track project progress, resource utilization, and performance metrics.

5. **Integration Capabilities:**
   - The ability to integrate with other software applications (e.g., CRM, ERP, accounting software) is crucial for seamless workflows and data synchronization.
6. **Mobile Accessibility:**
   - Consider tools that offer mobile applications, allowing team members to access project information and collaborate on-the-go.
7. **Support and Training:**
   - Look for vendors that provide comprehensive support and training resources to help your team maximize the tool's potential.

Tips for Selecting the Right Tools

1. **Assess Team Needs:**
   - Identify the specific needs of your project team, including collaboration requirements, task management, reporting, and resource allocation.
2. **Evaluate Budget:**
   - Consider your budget constraints and evaluate whether the tool offers good

value for its features. Many tools offer tiered pricing based on functionality.
3. **Involve the Team:**
    - Involve team members in the selection process to gather input and ensure buy-in. Their insights can help identify the most suitable tools.
4. **Trial and Testing:**
    - Take advantage of free trials or demo versions to test the tool's functionality and user experience before making a commitment.
5. **Research Reviews and Ratings:**
    - Look for reviews and ratings from other users to gain insights into the tool's strengths and weaknesses.
6. **Consider Scalability:**
    - Choose tools that can grow with your organization and accommodate future projects or increasing team sizes.
7. **Check for Security Features:**
    - Ensure that the tool has adequate security measures in place to protect sensitive project information and data.

Conclusion

The right tools and software can significantly enhance project management capabilities, improving collaboration, tracking, and overall project success. By understanding the various categories of project management tools and their features, project managers can make informed decisions that align with their team's needs and organizational goals. As technology continues to evolve, staying updated on the latest tools and best practices will empower project teams to navigate the complexities of modern projects effectively. In the next chapter, we will explore emerging trends in project management and how they are shaping the future of the profession.

Chapter 20: The Future of Project Management

As the landscape of work continues to evolve, so too does the field of project management. Emerging trends, technologies, and methodologies are reshaping how projects are planned, executed, and evaluated. This chapter explores the key factors influencing the future of project management, including technological advancements, changing workforce dynamics, evolving methodologies, and the growing importance of sustainability and agility.

Technological Advancements

1. **Artificial Intelligence and Automation:**
    - AI is increasingly being integrated into project management tools, automating routine tasks such as scheduling, resource allocation, and progress tracking. AI-driven analytics can provide insights into project performance and help predict potential risks.
    - Automation can streamline workflows, allowing project managers to focus on strategic decision-making rather than administrative tasks.

2. **Collaboration Tools and Remote Work:**
    - The rise of remote work has accelerated the adoption of collaboration tools that facilitate communication and teamwork across geographically dispersed teams. Tools like Slack, Microsoft Teams, and Zoom have become essential for maintaining connections and ensuring productivity.
    - Future project management will likely prioritize digital collaboration platforms that enhance engagement and coordination among remote teams.
3. **Data Analytics and Reporting:**
    - The ability to analyze data in real-time is transforming project management. Advanced analytics tools enable project managers to track KPIs, measure performance, and derive insights from past projects to improve future decision-making.
    - Predictive analytics can help identify potential project risks before they escalate, allowing for proactive management strategies.
4. **Blockchain Technology:**
    - Blockchain offers enhanced transparency and security in project management, especially in industries requiring strict compliance and accountability. It can

streamline processes such as contract management and payment verification, reducing disputes and enhancing trust among stakeholders.

Evolving Methodologies

1. **Agile and Hybrid Approaches:**
   - Agile methodologies continue to gain popularity across various industries due to their flexibility and responsiveness to change. The future of project management will see a greater emphasis on agile practices, allowing teams to adapt to evolving project requirements quickly.
   - Hybrid project management approaches, combining elements of traditional and agile methodologies, will become increasingly common, enabling teams to tailor their processes to the specific needs of each project.
2. **Emphasis on Outcomes and Value Delivery:**
   - The focus of project management is shifting from completing tasks on time and within budget to delivering measurable outcomes and value to stakeholders. This outcome-driven approach requires project managers to align project objectives with

organizational goals and stakeholder expectations.
3. **Design Thinking:**
    - Design thinking is an innovative methodology that emphasizes empathy, collaboration, and iterative problem-solving. Integrating design thinking into project management practices can enhance creativity and lead to better solutions that meet user needs.

Changing Workforce Dynamics

1. **Remote and Distributed Teams:**
    - The trend towards remote and distributed teams is likely to persist, necessitating project management strategies that prioritize virtual collaboration and communication.
    - Project managers will need to develop skills in leading diverse teams and managing cultural differences to foster effective collaboration.
2. **Focus on Employee Well-being:**
    - The well-being of team members is becoming a priority in project management. Future leaders will need to cultivate a supportive work environment that promotes mental health, work-life balance, and professional development.

- This focus on well-being can enhance team morale and productivity, leading to better project outcomes.
3. **Skill Development and Continuous Learning:**
    - The rapid pace of technological change requires project managers to engage in continuous learning and skill development. Upskilling in areas such as data analytics, AI, and agile methodologies will be essential for staying relevant in the field.

Sustainability and Social Responsibility

1. **Sustainable Project Management:**
    - There is a growing emphasis on sustainability in project management, with organizations increasingly prioritizing environmentally responsible practices. This includes assessing the environmental impact of projects, utilizing sustainable resources, and implementing green project management practices.
    - Future project managers will need to incorporate sustainability into their planning and decision-making processes, aligning projects with broader organizational sustainability goals.

2. **Corporate Social Responsibility (CSR):**
   - As stakeholders become more conscious of social responsibility, project managers will be expected to integrate CSR into their projects. This involves considering the social and ethical implications of project outcomes and ensuring that projects benefit the communities in which they operate.

The Role of Project Managers in the Future

1. **Leadership and Emotional Intelligence:**
   - The future of project management will require leaders who possess strong emotional intelligence, allowing them to navigate complex team dynamics, foster collaboration, and motivate diverse groups of individuals.
2. **Strategic Thinking:**
   - Project managers will need to adopt a strategic mindset, focusing on aligning projects with organizational goals and understanding the broader business context in which they operate.
3. **Adaptability and Resilience:**
   - As projects become more complex and unpredictable, project managers must be adaptable and resilient, capable of responding to changing circumstances and navigating challenges effectively.

Conclusion

The future of project management is characterized by rapid technological advancements, evolving methodologies, changing workforce dynamics, and a growing focus on sustainability and social responsibility. To thrive in this dynamic environment, project managers must embrace innovation, prioritize collaboration, and continuously develop their skills. By staying ahead of emerging trends and adapting to the needs of their teams and organizations, project managers can position themselves as strategic leaders capable of driving project success in an ever-changing landscape. As we move forward, the project management profession will continue to evolve, offering exciting opportunities for growth, learning, and impact.

www.ingramcontent.com/pod-product-compliance
Lightning Source LLC
Chambersburg PA
CBHW062106220526
45471CB00010B/3627